# Treasury of Smocking Designs

by

## Allyne S. Holland

Illustrations by Mark Cunningham

Dover Publications, Inc.
New York

# acknowledgments

*I thank my wonderful family for sparing me the time to write, stitch and teach. To Sandra Shield, who many years ago suggested I teach smocking, I express sincerest appreciation. My students have been diligent and invaluable in helping me compile this book. Barbara Owen, Garrie Daly, Jeanne Freund, Alma Baxter, Phyllis Dazet, Lynne Chambers, Joan West, Elaine Kelly and Sue Patton all deserve very special mention and thanks. Mark Cunningham was most skillful in preparing the beautiful artwork and made this work complete.*

Allyne Holland is an embroidery designer, teacher and author, certified on the advanced level by the Valentine Museum. She is the author of *A Guide to English Smocking* and *A Handbook for Smocking Teachers*. She has taught smocking and other types of needlework for many years and has studied smocking extensively in the United States and England. She is former national President of the Smocking Arts Guild of America.

Mark Cunningham is a technical and commercial illustrator. A graduate of V.P.I., he currently owns his own business, "Technical Graphics," in Richmond, Virginia.

*Treasury of Smocking Designs* is a new work, first published by Dover Publications, Inc., in 1985.

**Library of Congress Cataloging in Publication Data**

Holland, Allyne S.
  Treasury of smocking designs.

  (Dover needlework series)
  ISBN-13: 978-0-486-24991-9 (pbk.)
  ISBN-10: 0-486-24991-3 (pbk.)
  1. Smocking. I. Title. II. Series.
TT840.H67   1985      746.44              85-15905

Manufactured in the United States by Courier Corporation
24991310
www.doverpublications.com

# CONTENTS

# Smocking Traditions

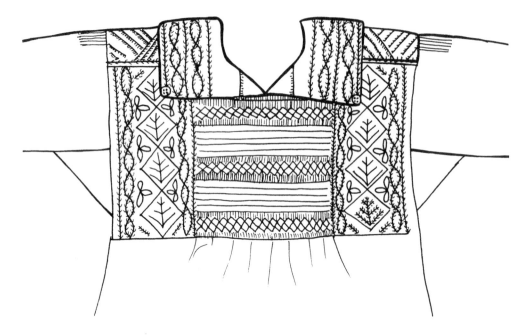

An English countryman of the late eighteenth or early nineteenth century would be amazed to see how smocking has changed today. The early traditional smock, with its geometric smocking and embroidered motifs, was seen as one walked down a country road or visited a rural marketplace in England or Wales, for this beautiful form of embroidery originally adorned the clothing of men who toiled in the fields, tended flocks of sheep, cut wood or led wagons and carts.

The smock (an old English term for shift or chemise) was a loose-fitting garment characterized by evenly gathered pleats on the body and sleeves. The pleats were held in place by simple embroidery stitches. A typical laborer's smock from the late eighteenth or early nineteenth century was made of linen, homespun or holland cloth, with the embroidery worked in matching linen thread.

While most smocks were made in natural shades, some geographic areas of England were known for their colors. In Derby smocks were often seen in blue, in Surrey and Sussex brown was the preferred color, while in Herefordshire they used green. Occasionally, a black smock was seen. For many years it was believed that the embroidered symbols on the garments represented the occupation of the owner. An extensive study carried out in 1962 and reported by Anne Buck in *Folklife* (Vol I, 1963) found no definite evidence of a connection between embroidery and occupation. In my own visits and study of smock collections in England, I found this to be true. It is not unusual to see several smocks that are identical and obviously made by a professional smock-maker, but the story adds considerably to the romance of the garment and so persists.

The early smocks were created by the working classes and little information has been passed on to us, since it is only in recent years that costume historians have paid much attention to the peasant smock. Although smocks were made by women, they were nearly always worn by men. Smocks were passed down from father to son, and worn and reworn until they were threadbare and could be patched no more. Because of this, few of these early working-class garments have survived. The earliest surviving decorated smock is from Mayfield in Sussex, dated 1779. It is in the collection of the Victoria and Albert Museum.

The smock stayed in general use in rural England until the early part of this century, when machine-made fabrics became available and were so inexpensive that country people were able to afford them. The fullness of the smock and its heavy weight proved an encumbrance because it could not be worn safely around the new farm machinery available in the growing Industrial Revolution. Thus, the traditional peasant smock did not survive the advent of the Industrial Revolution and became a garment to be worn only on special occasions.

Prior to the mid-nineteenth century, the upper classes wore smocking on their undergarments. In famous paintings, one can often see decorative gatherings peeking from a lady's bodice and sleeves. Young boys often wore the traditional-style smock, and by the 1880's, boys and girls wore fashionable smocked outfits.

In the 1880's patterns began to appear in *The Delineator* magazine, a major fashion and pattern magazine strongly influenced by Paris styles. In the late 1800's and early 20th century, patterns for fine embroidery and smocking were to be found in such popular publications as *Home Needlework Magazine*. During the 1920's many loose-fitting, "flapper-style" dresses were smocked at the waist. From the 1930's to the present, smocked garments rose and fell in popularity.

Today, as we nostalgically cast an eye to a simpler century, smocking has once again emerged and is enjoying its greatest period of popularity. While children's clothing remains the best-known use of smocking, many people are now developing designs in adult clothing and household accessories. Besides the basic stitches used in traditional combinations, smockers now use them in unconventional ways to create appealing shapes such as ducks, teddy bears, boats, elephants or fire engines. Further developments are the use of larger, free-form motifs such as landscapes, and the combination of smocking with other forms of needlework such as quilting, hemstitching and pulled thread. Better and more varied materials, not to mention a wider selection of colors, are now available to those who wish to improve their skills and explore new avenues of design. Shops specializing in smocking materials are more in evidence, and many a needlework department has added this old technique to its line. The Smocking Arts Guild of America (c/o The Cate Corporation, 1980 Isaac Newton Square South, Reston, Virginia 22090) provides a national link for those interested in this traditional art form. In England smockers can find a kindred soul with The Smocking Group of The Embroiderers' Guild (Apartment 41A, Hampton Court Palace, East Molesey, Surrey, England, UK).

As with any form of needlework or art, one is limited only by one's imagination, creative ability and ingenuity.

For a complete history of smocking, read Diana Keay's *The Book of Smocking* (New York: Arco, 1985). Maggie Hall has documented smock-making itself in her charming little book *Smocks* (Aylesbury, England: Shire Publications, Ltd., 1979).

# GENERAL INSTRUCTIONS

## Materials

**Fabrics:** In the United States, smocking is usually worked on soft fabrics such as batiste, cotton, cotton-polyester blends, silk and crêpe de Chine. Linen is also an excellent choice, be it fine or heavy, as are challis, wool, corduroy and velvet, although the latter are more suitable to the colder climate of the northern United States and Canada. If a fabric can be pleated by hand or machine without difficulty, it is suitable for smocking. Patterned fabrics such as gingham, striped fabric and that with dots can be used without pleating the fabric before smocking it.

Some fabrics pose problems in pleating which can be solved by spraying them on the wrong side with sizing before pleating.

**Threads:** Stranded cotton or embroidery floss is the most popular for smocking, but the thread should be compatible with the fabric. Pearl cotton works nicely on heavier fabrics and you should use linen on linen fabric and silk on silks and soft polyesters. For variety and more creativity in smocking, try the brightly colored rayon Brazilian fibers or some of the metallic threads available.

**Needles:** Fabrics, needles and threads must be compatible. As a general rule, for most soft fabrics such as cotton and cotton-polyester blends, use a No. 8 or a No. 10 crewel embroidery needle. With a No. 8 needle, use three strands of embroidery floss; with a No. 10 needle, use one or two strands. When using heavier embroidery thread such as pearl cotton or linen, use a chenille needle with a larger eye.

## Fabric Preparation

Proper preparation of any project for smocking is essential. Begin by washing and ironing all washable fabrics to remove unnecessary sizing. Plan the project carefully before pleating and beginning smocking. Generally, you will need three inches of fabric for every inch of the finished smocked piece, but the weight of the fabric and the smocking design will determine exactly how much fabric you will need. Cut off all selvage edges as they sometimes shrink and pucker. Be sure that the fabric is straight by pulling a thread and cutting along the pulled thread. If transfer dots are used, iron them onto the wrong side of the fabric, and use the exact number of rows to be smocked. Use a warm, not hot, iron, and do not slide the iron back and forth.

Use regular sewing or quilting thread in a contrasting color for gathering. Work an extra gathering row at both the top and bottom; these extra rows are usually worked with thread the same color as the fabric. Pull the pleats up to 1″ smaller than the desired finished size. Tie the gathering threads at the left, tying two or three rows together. On the right-hand side, leave the threads four or five inches long and hanging freely to allow for adjusting the pleats. You may need to leave longer threads on some projects. If you are left-handed, tie the threads at the right, leaving them free at the left.

After pleating, gently steam the pleats to set them in place. As you are steaming, pull the pleats at the top and bottom to straighten them. Do not place the iron directly on the pleats, but hold it slightly above the fabric. Allow the fabric to dry completely before beginning the embroidery.

Remember, beautiful smocking depends on correct preparation, with special attention to all details.

## Embroidery

Use 15″ to 18″ lengths of thread for embroidery. Thread has a nap, just as fabrics do, and can be felt to be smoother in one direction than the other. Always work with the nap pointing down. If the thread used is in multiple strands wrapped together (such as embroidery floss), separate the strands and place them together again before smocking. This step assures better coverage in any embroidery. Be sure that the nap on each strand is pointing down and keep the threads evenly adjusted in the needle. If two strands of thread are needed, do not double the thread in the needle; use two separate strands.

When beginning, come out on the side of the first pleat, then pick up the second pleat. Do not stitch into

The proper way to hold the fabric for smocking.

the first pleat twice. Be sure to pick up the same amount (about one-third) of each pleat, and keep the needle parallel to the gathering threads. Use your needle as a guide and line it up with the previous stitch, which it must match. Hold the fabric so that the pleats are evenly adjusted and vertical throughout. As you stitch across the piece, you can roll the fabric toward the back to give you a better grip on the piece. Develop an even tension. As you pull the pleats up, be sure that the stitch is in place before giving the final gentle tug.

Use a double knot or double backstitch when beginning and ending off. The double backstitch is strong enough not to unravel and is preferred by those experienced in embroidery. Cut the ends of the thread on the back of the work ¼″ long. Any knots used should be neat and small and not bulky.

Embroidery threads may be carried on the wrong side of the work by moving up and down in a zigzag fashion, catching the pleats in a herringbone stitch (page 12), then bringing the thread to the front again as needed. When carrying unused thread on the wrong side, do not skip more than three or four horizontal pleats. When thread must be carried further, it is best to end off and begin again at the appropriate pleat.

If it is difficult to pull the needle and thread through the fabric, either the eye of the needle is the wrong size, or too many threads are being used. When the needle and thread are making too large a hole in the fabric, a needle with a smaller eye and/or fewer threads will correct the problem.

While embroidering, be sure to study the stitch diagrams carefully. Stitch a small practice sampler first to be sure you understand the design and can spot any problem areas. You may also see some ways in which you can alter the design to personalize it. Be as creative as you can be.

Smocking, like any form of embroidery, is best when you have time to enjoy it!

## Finishing

After carefully checking your smocking design, gently remove all gathering threads except the top gathering row. Place the smocked piece right side down on a clean white towel. Extend the piece to the desired width and pin it to the towel. Use a ruler in measuring, rather than guessing. Be sure your iron is clean. Steam the piece lightly with an iron. *Never iron (press down on) any piece of smocking.* Use a gentle touch as any smocking stretches easily.

# Bibliography

### Historical Smocking

Armes, Alice, *English Smocks*. Leicester, England: The Dryad Press, 7th Edition, 1977.

Buck, Anne, "The Countryman's Smock." *Folklife* (magazine), Vol. 1, 1963.

Cave, Oenone, *Traditional Smocks and Smocking*. London: Mills and Boon, Ltd., 1979. (Reprint: *English Folk Embroidery*, 1965).

Hall, Maggie, *Smocks*. Aylesbury, England: Shire Publications, Ltd., 1979.

Hart, Natalie, *English Peasant Smocking*. New York: 1973.

Hughes, Therle, *English Domestic Needlework*. New York: Macmillan Co., 1961.

Marshall, Beverly, *Smocks and Smocking*. Sherborne, Dorset, England: Alphabooks, 1980.

Morris, Barbara, *Victorian Embroidery*. London: Herbert Jenkins, 1962.

*Priscilla Smocking Book*. Boston, Mass.: The Priscilla Publishing Co., 1916. (Now available in reprint from: The Tower Press, Inc., P.O. Box 428, Seabrook, NH 03874.)

Snook, Barbara, *English Historical Embroidery*. London: B.T. Batsford, 1960.

*Weldon's Practical Needlework*. No. 88, 1932, IPC, London.

### Smocking Techniques

Dean, Audrey Vincente, *Smocking, A Practical Beginner's Guide*. London: Stanley Paul & Co., Ltd., 1983.

Durand, Dianne, *Complete Book of Smocking*. New York: Van Nostrand Reinhold Co., 1982.

Durand, Dianne, *Smocking: Technique, Projects and Designs*. New York: Dover Publications, Inc., 1979.

Holland, Allyne, *A Guide to English Smocking*. Richmond, Va.: 1981.

Keay, Diana, *The Book of Smocking*. New York: Arco Pub., Inc., 1985. (Contains comprehensive history of smocking and how-to information.)

Knott, Grace L., *The Art of English Smocking*. Toronto, Canada: Thomas Allen, Ltd., 1975.

Thornton, Chella, *The Chella Thornton Smocking Book*. Montreal, Canada: Whitcombe and Gilmour, Ltd., 1951.

Thom, Margaret, *Smocking in Embroidery*. London: B.T. Batsford, Ltd., 1972.

Wilson, Erica, *Erica Wilson's Smocking*. New York: Charles Scribner's Sons, 1977.

# Stitches

Traditional English smocking is built around four groups of stitches:

    Straight Stitches
    Wave Stitches
    Combination Rows
    Decorative or Accent Embroidery Stitches

NOTE: On the stitch details shown, the gray area represents the valley of the pleat.

## Straight Stitches

In this category are outline, stem and cable stitches and their various combinations. Curved lines can be formed by using straight stitches; the lines may wave, intertwine or form scallops.

### Outline Stitch

This is a very attractive stitch that is useful in creating unusual designs and combinations, and is therefore especially suitable for contemporary smocking. It is worked in the same manner as in surface embroidery and must be worked very carefully to insure the effect of a neat, even line. Working parallel to the gathering thread and from left to right, pick up each pleat with the thread positioned above the needle. Work the stitches with the pleats close together and pull the thread fairly snugly. Cut the thread long enough to complete one section without a change. The floss will tend to knot and tangle as you work, so untwist the thread every few stitches to correct this.

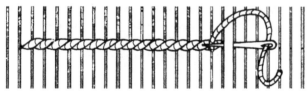

Outline Stitch

### Stem Stitch

This stitch is worked in the same manner as the outline stitch, but with the thread held below the needle. The individual stitches are not as clear as with the outline

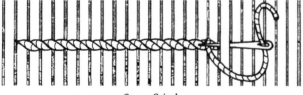

Stem Stitch

stitch, and a line of stem stitch will appear thinner than a line of outline stitch.

The outline and stem stitches are very similar in appearance—both form a continuous "rolled" line. In outline stitch, this roll forms toward the top of the line; in stem stitch, it forms toward the bottom of the line. Which of the two stitches to use in a given situation is a matter of personal preference.

### Wheat Stitch

The outline and stem stitches worked together form the Wheat Stitch. You may begin with either outline stitch or stem stitch.

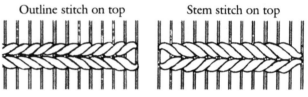

Wheat Stitch

### Cable Stitch

This stitch is worked left to right and parallel to the gathering thread. For the first stitch the thread is held below the needle; on the next stitch, the thread is held above the needle. By alternating the position of the thread on each stitch, the cable stitch is formed. As you work, pull the pleats together gently, giving each stitch a slight tug in the appropriate upward or downward position; at the same time, push the stitch into position with your thumbnail. Keep the stitch tension even throughout and see that no fabric shows under the embroidery.

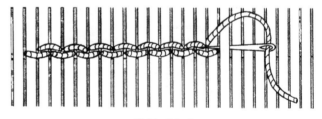

Cable Stitch

### Double Cable

Two parallel rows of cable stitch, both worked from left to right, form the double cable. The second row of stitches is positioned opposite to the first; that is, the first row begins in the stem-stitch position while the second row begins in the outline-stitch position (this is called an *Opposite Cable*). The stitches should lay neatly side by side, but should not overlap. Because the stitch resembles a chain, it is sometimes called *Chain Stitch*.

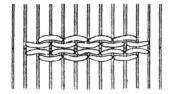

Double Cable

## Alternating Cable

This is a base row of cable stitch (dark thread in diagram) with a second row worked alternately above and below the base row.

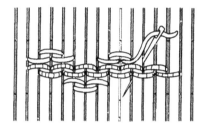

Alternating Cable

## Flowerettes or Cable Flowers

See section "Decorative or Accent Embroidery Stitches," below.

## Stacked Cables

Large areas of color can be filled in by working several rows of cable stitch, one on top of the other. Stacked cables are used primarily in picture smocking to create such motifs as teddy bears, ducks, sailboats, angels and baskets. Rows can be arranged as *Opposite Stacked Cables* (see double cable stitch for opposite cable), or they can be worked identically to each other (called *Parallel Stacked Cables*). The parallel stacked cable is very tight and has little elasticity; hence, the opposite stacked cable is usually the preferred stitch. To insure proper sizing when working stacked cables, stretch the pleats to the desired width before beginning to smock. Work the first row, then take the needle to the back of the fabric and turn the piece upside down to begin the next row. Technique is important here, for each stitch must line up perfectly with the previous row. When beginning a new row, be sure that the stitches are aligned and, where stitches line up, that the needle will come out at parallel points.

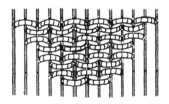

Opposite Stacked Cables

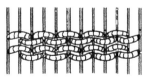

Parallel Stacked Cables

# WAVE STITCHES

Besides wave and trellis stitch, honeycomb, surface honeycomb, vanDyke and herringbone stitches belong to this division. All of these stitches form a zigzag pattern, and all of them can vary in size. A wave stitch worked between two rows of gathering threads is called a *Full-Space Wave*; a wave stitch worked halfway between two gathering threads is called a *Half-Space Wave*. Stitches may be worked as *parallels* (two or more identical rows) or as *opposites* (two or more rows with one row the mirror image of the next). Parallel wave stitches may be worked so closely together that no fabric shows (*Closed-Space Waves*) or in a more open formation (*Open-Space Waves*).

## Wave Stitch

This stitch (also known as *Diamond Stitch*) is worked from left to right with the needle parallel to the gathering threads.

To work a full-space wave, begin by bringing the needle out on the left side of the first pleat at the gathering thread. With the thread held below the needle, pick up the second pleat. With the thread still below the needle, move up to the next gathering thread and pick up the third pleat; then, with the thread held *above* the needle, pick up the fourth pleat. Move back down to the original gathering thread and, with the thread above the needle, pick up the next pleat. Continue in this way across the row. The top and bottom of the wave stitch are called by various names: point, closure, bridge or cable stitch. The half-space wave is worked in exactly the same way; only the spacing changes.

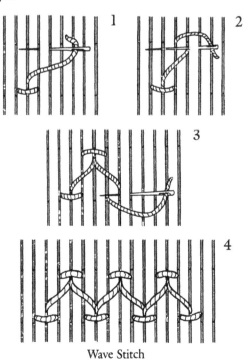

Wave Stitch

9

When rows of wave stitch are stitched as opposites, *Wave Diamonds* are formed; when rows of diamonds are stacked, they form *Latticework* or *Chevrons*. Wave stitch may also be worked to form heart and pyramid shapes.

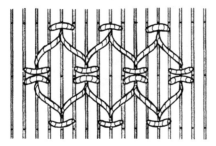

Wave Diamond

## Trellis Stitch

This is similar to and worked in the same manner as the wave stitch, but with one or more pleats picked up between the top and bottom points. It is usually worked on a half-space or a full-space level, although larger trellis stitches may be worked.

To form a basic full-space trellis, begin by bringing the needle out on the side of the first pleat at the gathering thread. With the thread held below the needle, pick up the second pleat; move up to halfway between the original gathering thread and the next gathering thread and pick up the third pleat; then move up to the next gathering thread and pick up the fourth pleat. Now, with the thread held *above* the needle, pick up the fifth pleat on the gathering thread; move down to mid-level and pick up the sixth pleat; then move down to the original gathering row and pick up the seventh pleat. Keep the needle parallel to the gathering threads at all times and be sure that the stitches on the left and right are properly aligned. Remember, when working up, keep the thread below the needle, when working down, keep the thread above the needle.

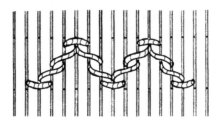

Trellis Stitch

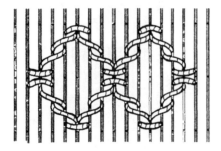

Trellis Diamond

A basic trellis, with only one pleat picked up between the top and the bottom, is also known as a *Quarter Wave*. Larger trellis stitches are formed by picking up more pleats between the bottom and top points.

Two rows of opposite trellis stitch form a *Trellis Diamond* and several rows of diamonds form the *Lattice Trellis*. Like the wave stitches, trellis stitches can be used to form hearts and pyramids.

## Honeycomb Stitch

This is the most elastic of all the smocking stitches and, as a result, requires less fabric than most other stitches. It is ideal to use on ginghams, stripes and dotted fabrics, for when the fabric design can be used as a guide, the stitch can be worked without pre-pleating the fabric.

Honeycomb stitch should be worked in a color thread that will not show through the fabric, since only a small satin-type stitch should show on the right side of the fabric.

Working from left to right, bring the needle out on the left side of the first pleat at the gathering thread. Pick up pleat 2 *and* pleat 1 at the same time and pull them together gently. Insert the needle on the right side of pleat 2 and, on the wrong side of the fabric, move down to the next gathering thread, bringing the needle out on the left side of pleat 2. Pick up pleats 3 and 2 and pull them together as before. Continue in this way across the row. When working at the top gathering row, the thread will be above the needle; at the bottom, the thread will be below the needle.

Honeycomb stitch can be worked in parallel rows to form waves or in opposite rows to form a diamond or lattice design. This stitch can also be effectively worked in pyramids.

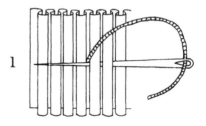

1

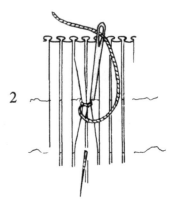

2

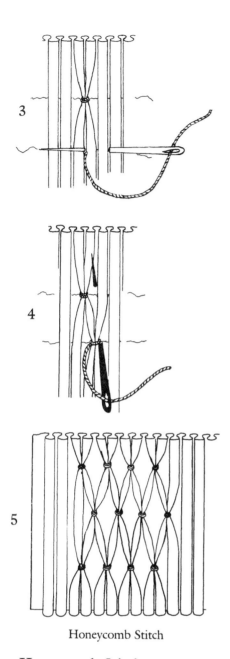

Honeycomb Stitch

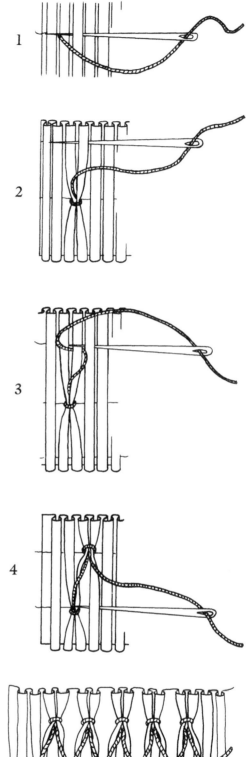

## Surface Honeycomb Stitch

This is worked similarly to the honeycomb; however, the thread between the satin stitches is left on the right side of the work.

Bring the needle out on the left side of the first pleat. With the thread held below the needle, pick up the second pleat and pull it to the first pleat. With the thread still below the needle, move up to the next gathering thread and pick up the top of the second pleat. With the thread held *above* the needle, pick up the third pleat and pull it to the second pleat. Move back down to the original gathering row and, with the thread above the needle, pick up the bottom of the third pleat. With the thread below the needle, pick up the fourth pleat. Continue across the row.

Like honeycomb stitch, surface honeycomb can be worked to form waves, diamonds, latticework or pyramids.

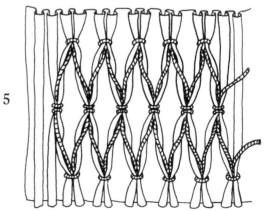

Surface Honeycomb Stitch

11

## Herringbone Stitch

Working from left to right, bring the needle out on the left side of the first pleat at the gathering thread. Move up to the next gathering thread and pick up the second pleat, then move back down to the original gathering thread to pick up the third pleat. Continue in this way across the row.

This stitch is often used to carry the thread across the wrong side of the fabric.

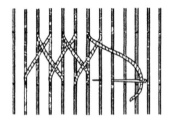

Herringbone Stitch

## VanDyke Stitch

The vanDyke stitch is similar to the honeycomb and surface honeycomb; however, it is one of the rare smocking stitches worked from right to left. It is often worked on gingham, with the fabric and thread colors matched.

Working from right to left, bring the needle out on the left of the second pleat from the starting point. With the thread held above the needle, pick up pleats 1 and 2 and pull them together. Move down to the next gathering thread and pick up pleats 2 and 3. With the thread below the needle, go through the same two pleats again. Move back up to the original gathering thread and pick up pleats 3 and 4. With the thread above the needle, go through both pleats again. Continue across the row.

If you are using this stitch in combination with stitches that are worked from left to right, you can make all of the stitches begin at the same edge of the fabric by turning the piece upside down to work the vanDyke stitch.

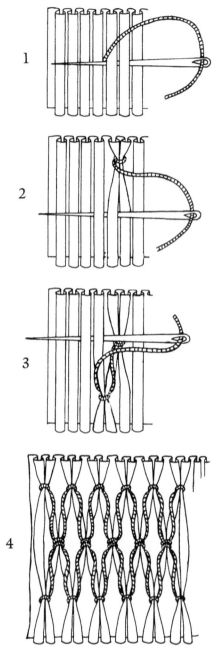

VanDyke Stitch

12

# Stitch Combinations

Stitch combinations include rows formed by combining several stitches. Diamonds, links, turrets, hearts, rectangles, triangles and all cross-over stitch combinations belong to this classification. Wave diamond, trellis diamond (both on page 10) and all latticework actually belong in this category, but the formation of these rows is more easily understood when the stitches are placed next to their parent constructions.

## Wave, Trellis and Cable Combinations

Wave and trellis stitches can be combined with cable stitches to form *Link* and *Diamond Combinations*.

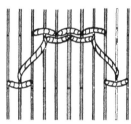

Cable-Wave Combination

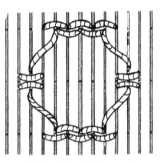

Cable-Wave Diamond

## Wheat Stitch Variation

This is formed by a combination of outline and stem stitch worked intermittently with wave diamonds. Outline stitch is used on the top row and stem stitch on the bottom. There is no set number of outline and stem stitches, but it is most effective to use more than five and less than ten.

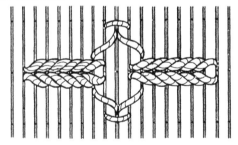

Wheat Stitch Variation

## Turret Stitch

This is a surface honeycomb stitch with a row of cable stitch above and below it.

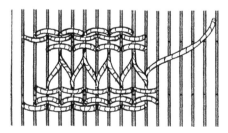

Turret Stitch

## Cross-Over Stitch Combinations

Cross-over stitch combinations are a challenge to work and can be used to create many exciting patterns. The variety of stitches is almost endless and the technique offers an entirely new perspective on smocking.

These stitch combinations are created by first laying a base row of stitches, then returning with a second row to fill in the spaces left open on the base row. The second row does not have to be the same stitch as the first, but it does have to be a stitch that will fit easily with the first and not overpower it. Cross-over stitch combinations work best when planned for an open, airy effect, for packed stitches do not give each row a chance to display itself. Avoid overworking any design.

One, two, or more colors may be used. Decorative stitches may be included, but they are usually unnecessary. When working with one color (white thread on a white background, for example), a lacy effect is achieved. Selecting a series of three related colors, such as three shades of rose, gives a subtle, shaded effect.

## Cable-Wave Cross-Over Stitch Combination

Work a base row of full-space cable-wave stitch with the point to the bottom (dark thread on diagram). In a contrasting color, work a second row of full-space cable-wave with the point to the top (lighter thread on diagram).

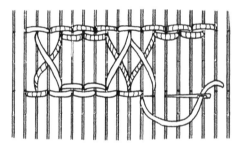

Cable-Wave Cross-Over
Stitch Combination

## Trellis Cross-Over Stitch Combination or Lace Stitch

Work a base row of full-space wave stitch (dark thread on diagram), skipping a pleat between the top and bottom levels, then work a row of trellis stitch, picking up the skipped pleat and thread from the base row (lighter thread on diagram).

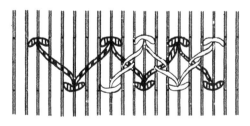

Trellis Cross-Over
Stitch Combination

# Decorative or Accent Embroidery Stitches

Embroidery stitches add a special touch to any smocking project. French knots, bullion-knot rosebuds, flowerettes, lazy daisy and satin stitches all belong to this category. In most cases, this additional embroidery is added after the main smocking is completed. To work decorative stitches successfully, spread the pleats out to the desired finished size. Use three strands of embroidery floss on regular fabric surfaces with a No. 8 crewel needle. On fine batiste, use one or two strands of floss with a No. 10 crewel needle. A milliner's needle is useful for working bullion knots.

When embroidering, pull the stitches snugly, but not too tightly. Work with a relaxed tension and take care that all stitches are uniform. When necessary, to prevent unsightly pull or distortion (such as might happen with the lazy daisy stitch), work a backstitch midway on the wrong side of the work, then proceed. On the few occasions that the thread must be carried more than 3 or 4 pleats, pick up a pleat with a small stitch above and below (in herringbone-stitch fashion) so that a zigzag pattern appears on the wrong side. For large areas of embroidery stitches, it may be necessary to backsmock the piece to hold the pleats together and prevent gaping holes around the embroidered areas. Use one or two strands of thread in the same color as the fabric, and work a cable, a wave or a trellis stitch (whatever is compatible with the rest of the design) on the wrong side of the fabric.

As with all embroidery, practice makes perfect. For those stitches not familiar to you, practice on linen with crewel yarn and a No. 24 chenille needle, or on muslin with embroidery floss and a No. 8 crewel needle. When practicing, it is best to work with fabric in an embroidery hoop.

## Flowerettes or Cable Flowers

These are formed by first working three cable stitches in one direction, then turning the fabric to work three more cable stitches opposite the first. The small space at the center gives the illusion of a tiny flower. A *Half-Flowerette* is formed when only three cable stitches are worked.

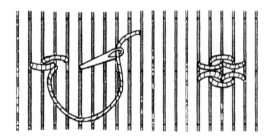

Flowerette or Cable Flower

## Satin Stitches

Embroidery stitches can be wrapped evenly over two or more pleats to create solid blocks of color. When working, lay stitches side by side, and do not overlap them. Also, take care that the thread does not twist. A *Satin Stitch Dot* is three stitches over two pleats. The *Satin Stitch Bar* is four or more stitches over two pleats. A *Spool* is worked over four pleats. These stitches work well for tree trunks, body shapes and stems.

Satin Stitch Dot    Satin Stitch Bar

## Lazy Daisy Stitch

This looped chain stitch is worked in the same manner as in surface embroidery. As it is easily pulled out of shape, take care to hold it in place while working each loop.

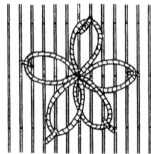

Lazy Daisy Flower

## Knotted Stitches

*Bullion Knots*, *French Knots* and *Long-Arm French Knots* are filling, or detached, stitches used to cover a specific area. In each case the thread is wrapped around the needle. To help a bullion-knot rosebud stay open, wrap the first stitch in one direction, then work the next stitch in the opposite direction. A true French knot has only one wrap. When a thicker knot is needed, use more strands of thread.

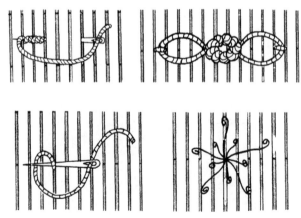

French Knot    Long-Arm French Knot

# Reference Glossary of Smocking Terms

*Accent:* A decorative embroidery stitch.

*Alternating Cable:* A row of cable with an additional row of cable stitch worked above and below it.

*Bar:* Four or more satin stitches.

*Base Row(s):* Row(s) worked first in a design to serve as the foundation.

*Bullion Knot:* An embroidery stitch often used to form rosebuds.

*Cable:* A straight stitch.

*Cable Diamonds:* Two rows of cable-wave or cable-trellis combination worked opposite one another.

*Cable-Wave:* A wave stitch formed with three or more cable stitches at the top and bottom of each wave.

*Chain:* Another name for a double cable.

*Closure:* The top or bottom of a wave or trellis stitch; also known as a point, bridge or cable.

*Combination Rows:* Rows formed by a series of stitches: diamonds, links, turrets and all cross-over stitch combinations.

*Cross-Over:* A row of wave, trellis or cable-wave worked with another row of the same (or compatible) stitch over the first; also known as a crisscross.

*Decorative Stitch:* An embroidery stitch used to highlight a design.

*Dot:* Three satin stitches.

*Double Cable:* Two rows of cable stitch worked opposite each other.

*Flowerette:* Two sets of three cable stitches worked opposite each other.

*French Knot:* A decorative embroidery stitch.

*Full-Space:* The space between two gathering threads.

*Gathering Threads:* Threads holding the pleats in place; also known as guide threads.

*Half-Space:* Space from midway between one gathering thread and the next gathering thread.

*Herringbone Stitch:* A wave stitch.

*Honeycomb:* A wave stitch worked so that small satin stitches appear on the surface.

*Latticework:* Rows of wave stitches smocked opposite each other to form a chevron or diamond pattern.

*Motif:* The central or dominant design element.

*Opposites:* Two or more rows, with one row the mirror image of the next.

*Outline:* A straight stitch.

*Parallels:* Two or more identical rows.

*Pyramid:* Stitches smocked to form the shape of a triangle.

*Rolling Outline Stitches:* Outline or stem stitch.

*Satin Stitch:* Stitches wrapped uniformly around a pleat; also known as dots, bars or spools, depending on the number of wraps.

*Spool:* A satin stitch.

*Stacked Stitches:* A series of stitches smocked one row on top of another to form a solid block of color; may be worked in cable, wave or trellis, in either opposite or parallel combinations.

*Stem:* A straight stitch.

*Straight Stitches:* Outline, stem or cable.

*Surface Honeycomb:* A wave stitch.

*Trellis:* A wave stitch.

*Turret:* A row of surface honeycomb worked between parallel rows of cable.

*VanDyke:* A wave stitch worked from right to left.

*Wave:* A stitch that forms a zigzag pattern.

*Wheat Stitch:* A combination of outline and stem stitches.

# Smocking Graphs

Part of the current smocking rage stems from the development of new methods to reproduce exact designs. By using graphs to portray stitches, designs can be duplicated.

On the graph, each side-to-side numbered horizontal line represents a gathering thread. A top-to-bottom vertical line represents a pleat. A slanted line on a graph (such as for trellis stitch) indicates that a pleat will be picked up at that point. The first (base) row(s) to be worked on any design is marked by an asterisk (*).

All graphs are designed for right-handed workers. Left-handed smockers need simply to turn the graphs upside down.

## Stitch Key

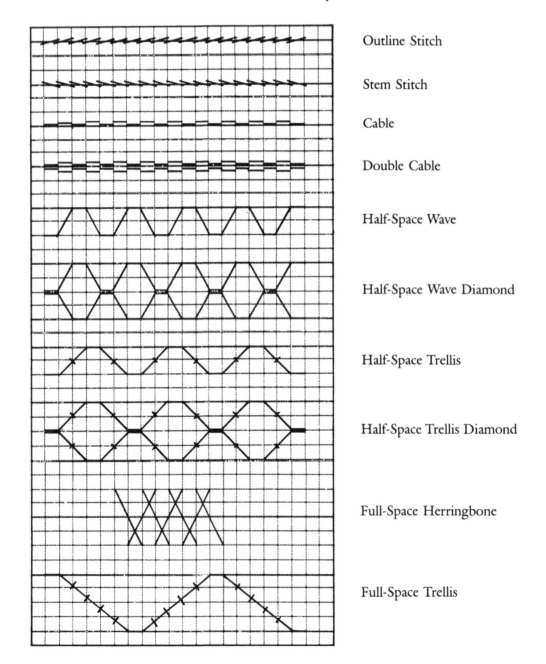

Outline Stitch

Stem Stitch

Cable

Double Cable

Half-Space Wave

Half-Space Wave Diamond

Half-Space Trellis

Half-Space Trellis Diamond

Full-Space Herringbone

Full-Space Trellis

# Smocking Designs
## Group 1: Geometric Smocking
### (Intermediate Skill)

The smocking ideas presented here are for someone who is more than a beginner, but less than an expert. Try your hand at the designs as shown, then consider developing them further with color changes, the addition of decorative stitches, and the like. With two exceptions, the designs shown are of sample swatches. Any and all would make a smashing yoke, a pretty pocket for a favorite blouse or an evening bag for that special occasion when you want to show off your considerable talents.

# Victorian Memories

**Row 2 to 1½ and Row 2 to 2½:** Work half-space cable-wave diamond first. Then work half-flowerettes, carrying thread loosely across back of work as indicated by arrows; the order in which half-flowerettes are to be worked is indicated by the small numbers.

**Row 5½ to 6½:** Decorative stitches. Work bullion-knot rosebuds of three knots each—outer knots in pale pink, center knot in pink; add two green lazy daisy leaves to each rosebud.

### Color Key

A  Blue          C  Pink
B  Pale Pink     D  Green

*Shown in color on inside front cover*

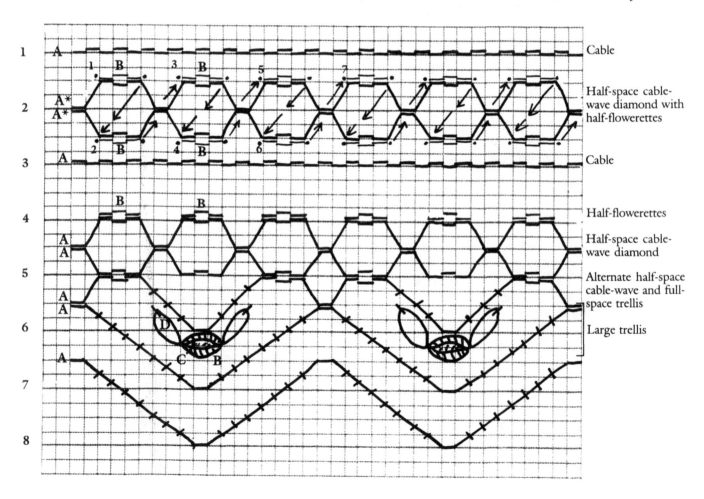

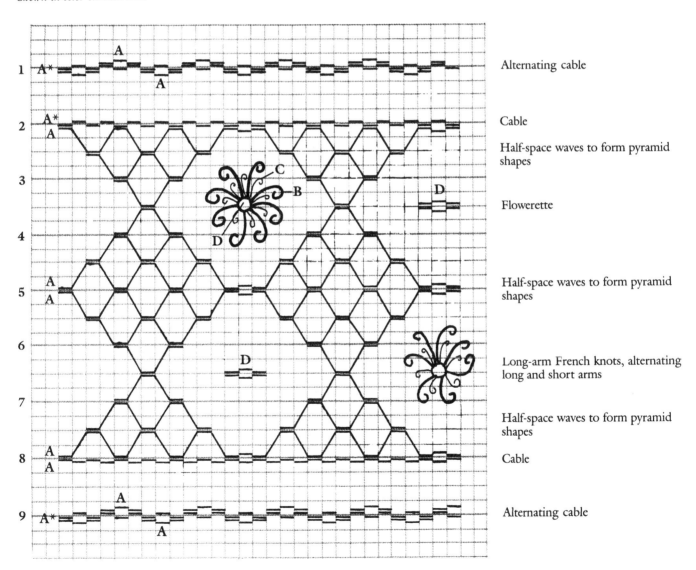

*Shown in color on back cover*

# Amy Louise

**Decorative Stitches:** Do not bring all long-arm French knots out of the same hole, as this will damage fabric. At the center of each flower, work a French knot with light peach.

**Variation:** To enlarge the design, repeat the central part of the motif between Rows 3½ and 6½.

### Color Key
A   Blue                C   Dark Peach
B   Medium Peach        D   Light Peach

1   A*
    A                                             Alternating cable

2   A*                                            Cable
    A
                                                  Half-space waves to form pyramid
                                                  shapes
3                                                 C
                                              B
                                                  Flowerette
                                              D
4   D

5   A                                             Half-space waves to form pyramid
    A                                             shapes

6                                                 Long-arm French knots, alternating
    D                                             long and short arms

7                                                 Half-space waves to form pyramid
                                                  shapes

8   A                                             Cable
    A

9   A*                                            Alternating cable
    A

# Katie's Best

**Row 2 to 3 and Row 3 to 2:** Beginning at Row 2, skipping the middle pleat between the top and bottom gathering rows, work a base row of full-space cable-wave combination to Row 3. Beginning at Row 3, work a cross-over row of full-space cable-trellis combination to Row 2, picking up the center skipped pleat and the thread of the previous row.

**Center Motif:** Work a row of half-space trellis between Rows 5 and 4½, then between Rows 6 and 6½. Complete each heart shape by working a full-space trellis between Rows 6 and 5, following arrows for carrying thread at back of work. When taking thread to the back of the work and returning it to the front, insert the needle into the *side* of a pleat. Do not stitch into the valley as that will distort the stitch.

**Row 6½ to 7:** Decorative stitches. Work bullion-knot rosebuds of three knots each—outer knots in yellow, center knot in pale yellow; add two green lazy daisy stitch leaves to each rosebud.

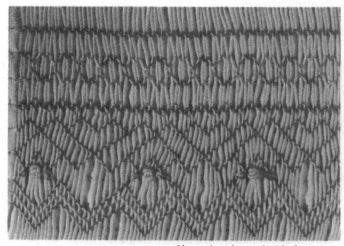

*Shown in color on inside front cover*

**Color Key**

| A | Green | B | Yellow | C | Pale Yellow |

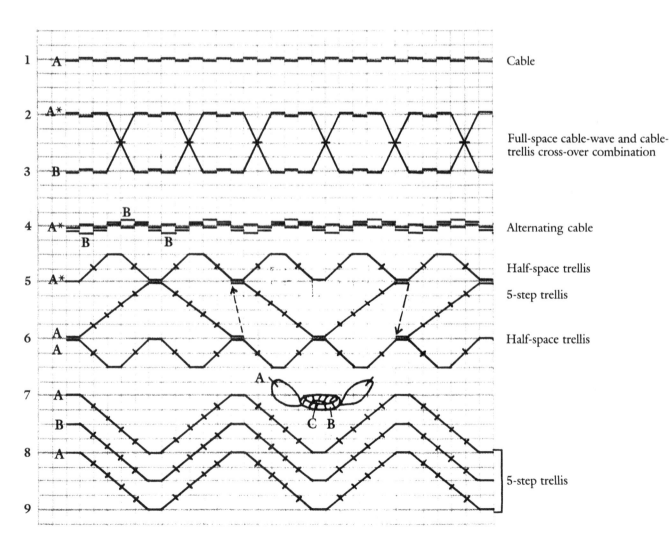

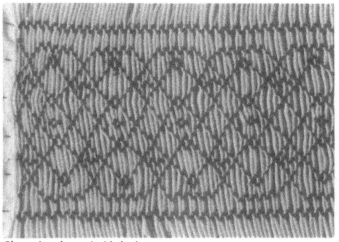

*Shown in color on inside back cover*

# A Touch of Spring

**Row 2½ to 2 and Row 4½ to 5:** Decorative stitches. Work a half-flowerette in first trellis diamond; carry thread on wrong side to top of next cable-trellis diamond and work another half-flowerette. Continue across in this manner.

**Row 3½:** Decorative stitches. Work a flowerette in each cable-trellis diamond.

**Variations:** This design can be enlarged by expanding the motif and/or by adding borders. For a bishop yoke, add three rows of large trellis spaced over two or three gathering threads, depending on the desired depth.

**Color Key**

A  Blue     B  Green     C  Peach

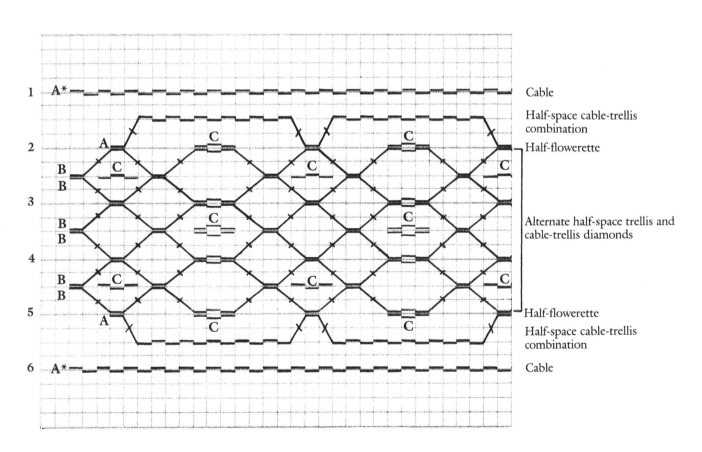

# Jessica

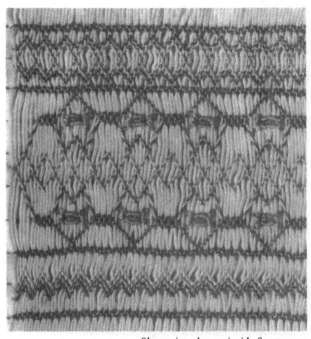

**Center Motif:** Work the base row of trellis diamonds between Rows 5 and 6. Work the alternate half-space and full-space cable-trellis combinations between Rows 5 and 4 and between Rows 6 and 7, then add the cable and 5-step trellis combination between Rows 3¼ and 4 and Rows 7¼ and 8.

**Row 4 and Row 7:** Decorative stitches. Work bullion-knot rosebuds of 3 bullion knots each—outer knots in medium rose, center knot in dark rose. Leaves are lazy daisy stitch.

**Variation:** This border may be expanded for a large yoke by adding more rows of half-space trellis through the center to form a larger lattice.

### Color Key

| | | | |
|---|---|---|---|
| A | Dark Rose | C | Light Rose |
| B | Medium Rose | D | Green |

*Shown in color on inside front cover*

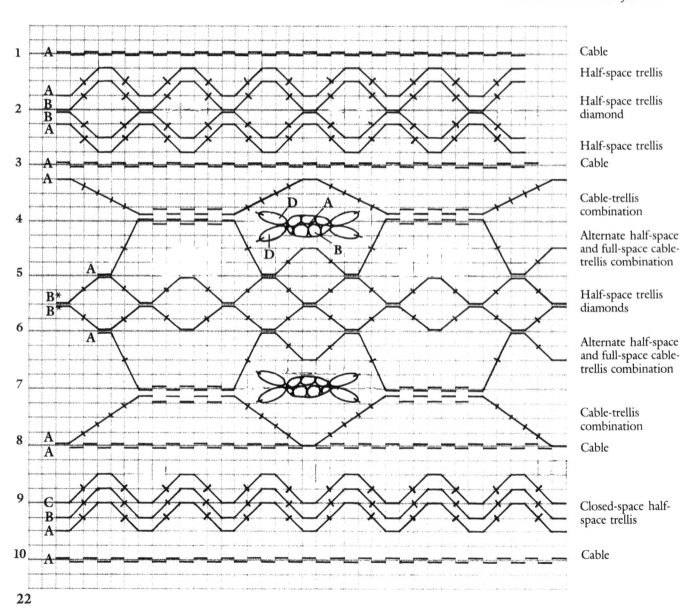

# CARRIE ANN

**Row 6½:** Decorative stitches. In diamonds, work first a bullion-knot rosebud of 2 knots each, then a flowerette as indicated on graph.

**Variations:** This design is particularly suited for shading colors. The decorative stitches may be worked in either the hearts or the diamonds. For an alternative lower border, use a large trellis.

**Color Key**

A  Turquoise      B  Pink      C  Off-White

*Shown in color on inside back cover*

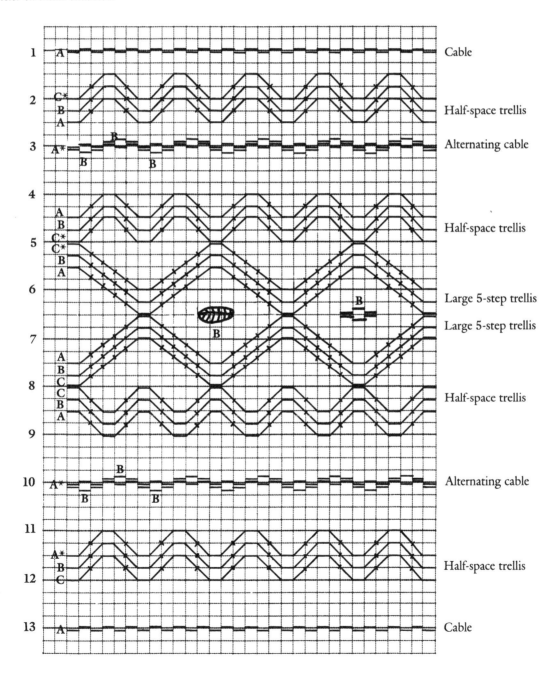

# Cynthia's Special Day

*Shown in color on inside front cover*

**Center Motif:** Work trellis and cable-trellis diamonds between Rows 6 and 9; the base row begins on Row 6½. Add cable-wave combination from Row 6 to 5 and Row 9 to 10.

**Row 5½ and Row 9½:** Decorative stitches. Alternate flowerettes and bullion-knot rosebuds with lazy daisy stitch leaves as indicated on graph.

**Additional decoration on pillow:** Seed pearls are scattered throughout the centers of the diamonds. Rosettes are of ¼"-wide double-faced satin ribbon; streamers and knotted bows are of the same ribbon. For the double-layer lace edging, use 1" lace over 2" lace. Pillow is made of 100% Swiss cotton batiste.

**Color Key**

Thread to match fabric for all stitching

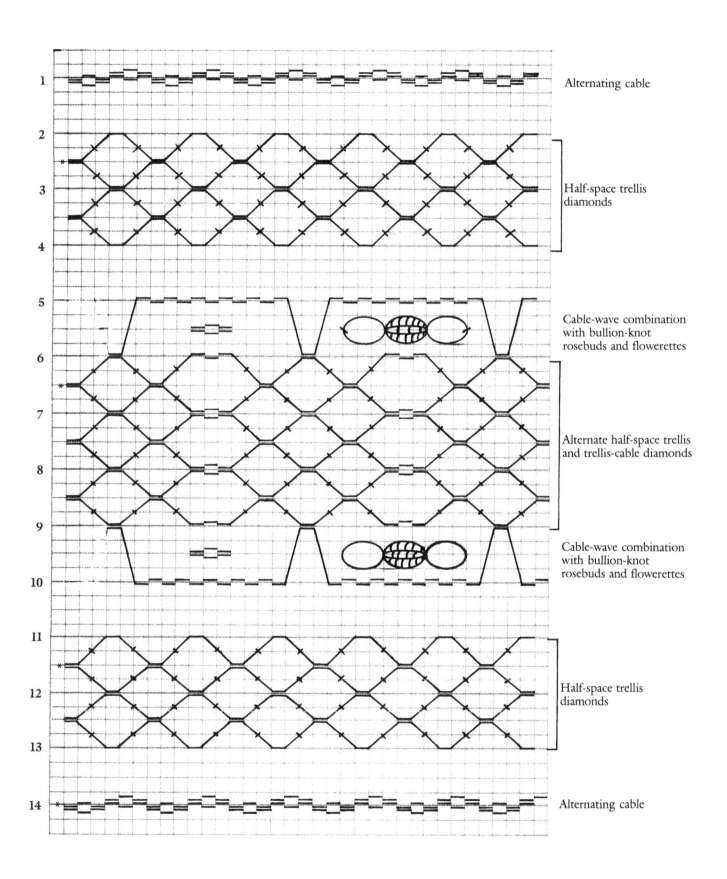

1 — Alternating cable

2
3 — Half-space trellis diamonds
4

5 — Cable-wave combination with bullion-knot rosebuds and flowerettes

6
7 — Alternate half-space trellis and trellis-cable diamonds
8

9 — Cable-wave combination with bullion-knot rosebuds and flowerettes
10

11
12 — Half-space trellis diamonds
13

14 — Alternating cable

# Indian Summer

*Shown in color on inside back cover*

**Row 6:** Work flowerettes at center of diamonds as indicated.

**Color Key**

A   Yellow        B   Orange        C   Green

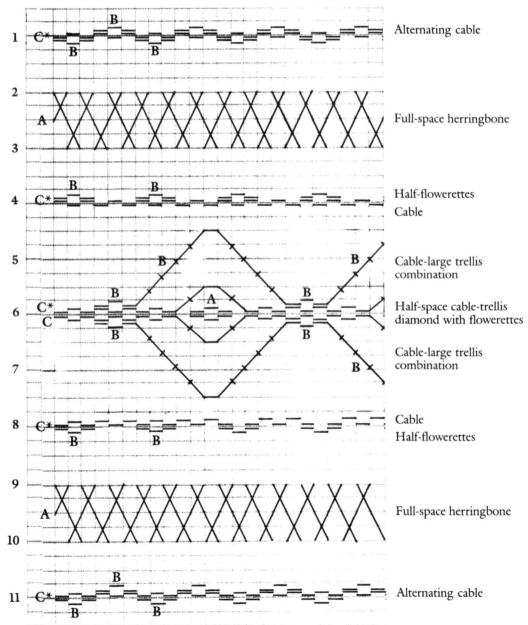

1   Alternating cable

2   Full-space herringbone
3

4   Half-flowerettes
    Cable

5   Cable-large trellis
    combination

6   Half-space cable-trellis
    diamond with flowerettes

7   Cable-large trellis
    combination

8   Cable
    Half-flowerettes

9   Full-space herringbone
10

11  Alternating cable

# GROUP 2:
## CROSS-OVER STITCH COMBINATIONS

*(Intermediate and Advanced Skills)*

Cross-over stitch combinations, with their interplay of colors and stitches and the resulting lace-like effects, add an interesting variation to any smocking design. A good suggestion here: With colored pencils, mark the lines for each color of thread on the graph. This one step will make following the design far easier.

These patterns should be attempted only by those who are strong intermediate or advanced smockers.

# Magic

**Row 1:** Begin cable with thread in stem-stitch position.

**Rows 1½ to 2½, 3½ to 2½, 3½ to 4½ and 5½ to 4½:** With rose, work base rows of cable-wave combination.

**Rows 2 to 1, 2 to 3, 4 to 3, 4 to 5 and 6 to 5:** With blue, work cross-over rows of cable-wave combination (dark lines on graph).

**Row 6:** Begin cable with thread in outline-stitch position.

**Variations:** To expand the motif, add a border of cables and wave diamond. Add alternating cables between borders and central motif. Flowerettes or satin stitches will fit nicely in any diamond.

**Color Key**

A   Rose   B   Blue

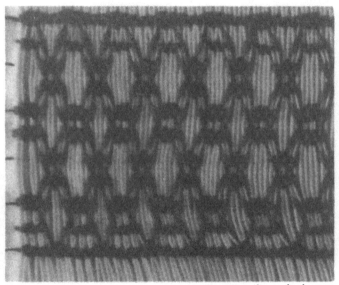

*Shown in color on back cover*

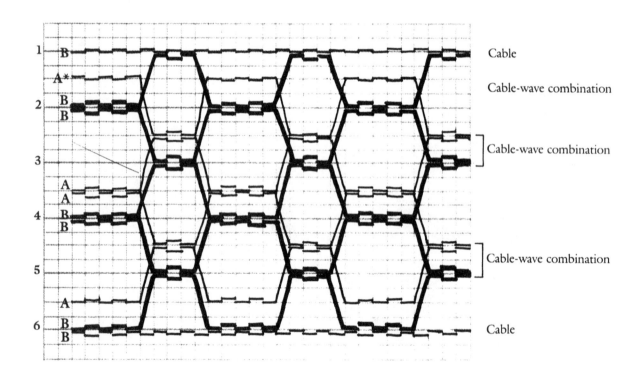

28

# ROSEMARY

## CENTER MOTIF

**Rows 6 to 7:** Work base rows of half-space trellis diamond in off-white.

**Rows 6 to 5½ and 7 to 7½:** With off-white, complete the tops of the diamonds in half-space trellis.

**Rows 6 to 4¼ and 7 to 9:** Work the large trellis in off-white.

**Cross-Over Rows:** With red, begin the large trellis (dark line on graph) at Row 4¼ and work down to Row 6, picking up both the pleat and the thread from the previous row. From the base of the first large trellis, carry the thread on the wrong side to the center of the first off-white diamond motif. Make a bullion-knot rosebud, then carry the yarn on the wrong side, bringing it out to begin the next large trellis. Continue in this way across the row. Work Rows 9 to 7 in the same way, omitting the rosebuds.

**Color Key**

A   Red        B   Off-White        C   Green

*Shown in color on inside front cover*

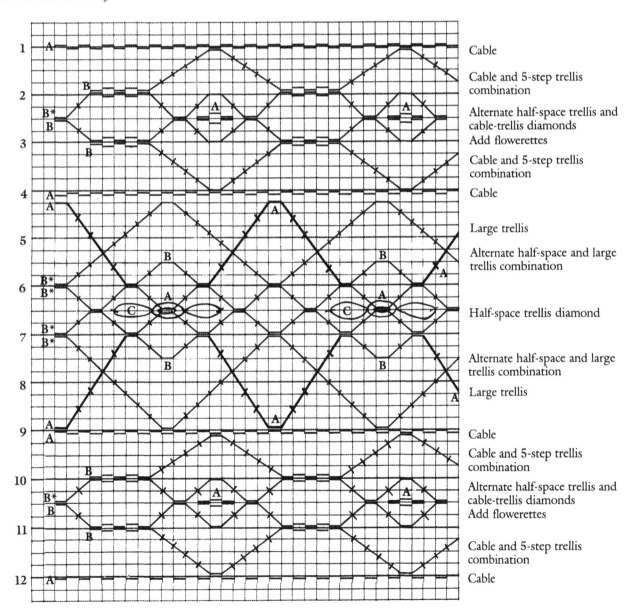

| | |
|---|---|
| 1 | Cable |
| 2 | Cable and 5-step trellis combination |
| | Alternate half-space trellis and cable-trellis diamonds |
| 3 | Add flowerettes |
| | Cable and 5-step trellis combination |
| 4 | Cable |
| 5 | Large trellis |
| | Alternate half-space and large trellis combination |
| 6 | Half-space trellis diamond |
| 7 | Alternate half-space and large trellis combination |
| 8 | Large trellis |
| 9 | Cable |
| | Cable and 5-step trellis combination |
| 10 | Alternate half-space trellis and cable-trellis diamonds |
| | Add flowerettes |
| 11 | Cable and 5-step trellis combination |
| 12 | Cable |

# Aurora

*Shown in color on inside front cover*

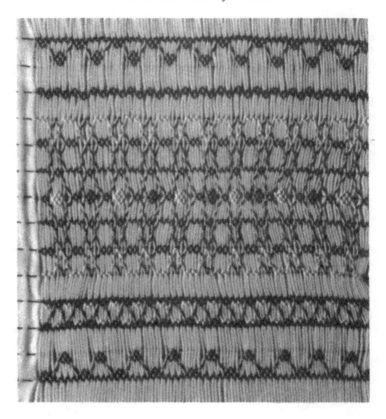

**Rows 1 to 2 and 14 to 13:** Work base rows of cable-wave combination in green. With pink, work half-flowerettes and stacked cables, turning the piece as necessary and carrying the thread on the wrong side of the work as indicated by the arrows.

### CENTER MOTIF

**Rows 5 to 4, 5 to 6, 9 to 8 and 9 to 10:** With green, work base rows of cable-wave combination, skipping the middle pleat between the top and bottom gathering threads on Rows 5 to 4 and 9 to 10. Work cross-over rows of cable-trellis combination (dark lines on graph) in pink or yellow as indicated, picking up the skipped pleat and the thread from the previous row.

**Rows 6 to 8:** With green, work cable-trellis diamonds.

**Rows 11 to 12:** With dark green, work cable at Row 11 beginning with the thread above the needle; work cable at Row 12 beginning with the thread below the needle. With yellow, work cable-wave combination between the rows of cable stitch; then work cross-over row of cable-wave combination (dark line on chart) with dark green.

**Row 7:** Decorative stitches. Spread pleats to desired finished width before beginning, then work stacked cable flowers, turning the work as necessary.

### Color Key

| A | Green | C | Yellow |
|---|-------|---|--------|
| B | Pink | D | Dark Green |

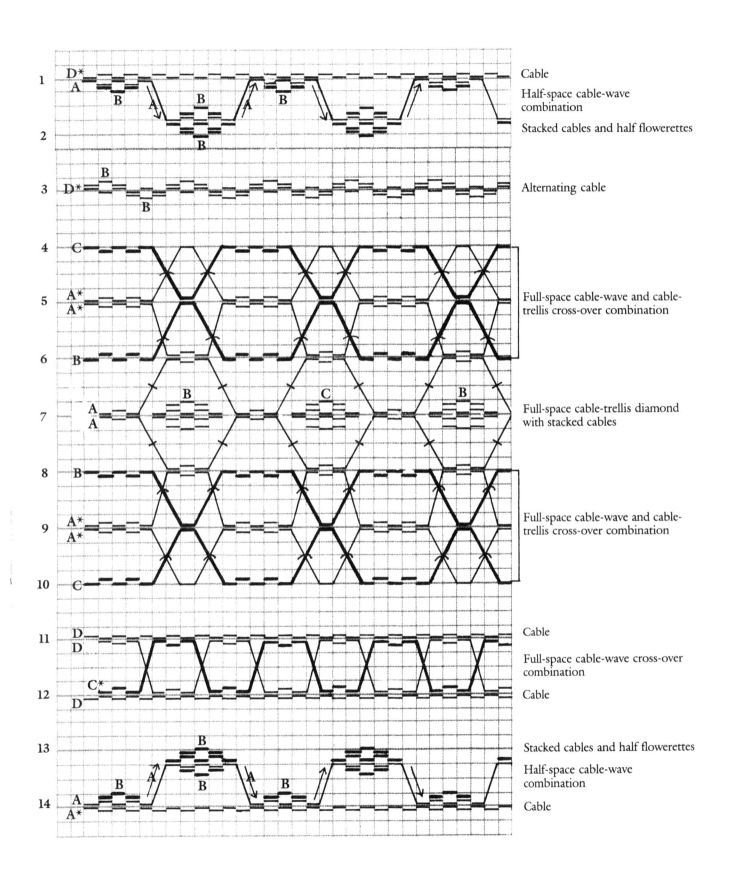

1 — Cable

Half-space cable-wave combination

2 — Stacked cables and half flowerettes

3 — Alternating cable

4
5 — Full-space cable-wave and cable-trellis cross-over combination
6

7 — Full-space cable-trellis diamond with stacked cables

8
9 — Full-space cable-wave and cable-trellis cross-over combination
10

11 — Cable

Full-space cable-wave cross-over combination

12 — Cable

13 — Stacked cables and half flowerettes

Half-space cable-wave combination

14 — Cable

# A Puzzled Heart

*Shown in color on inside front cover*

## TOP MOTIF

**Rows 2 to 1½ and 3 to 3½:** Work half-space waves in colors as indicated.

**Rows 2 to 3:** Beginning at Row 2 with green, work a 3-step trellis to complete the green hearts; then, beginning at Row 3 with red, work a 3-step trellis to complete the red hearts (dark line on graph).

## CENTER MOTIF

**Rows 5 to 4½, 6½ to 7, 7½ to 7 and 9 to 9½:** Work half-space waves in colors as indicated.

**Rows 5 to 6 and 9 to 8:** With white, work a 3-step trellis to complete the white hearts.

**Rows 6½ to 5½ and 7½ to 8½:** With red, work a 3-step trellis to complete the red hearts (dark lines on graph).

**Row 7:** Decorative stitches. With green, work 3 satin stitches in every other wave diamond.

## BOTTOM MOTIF

**Rows 11½ to 11 and 12½ to 13:** With green, work half-space waves.

**Row 11½ to 12½:** With green, work a 3-step trellis to complete the hearts. Add red flowerettes as indicated.

**Variation:** Study the design carefully to see how the shapes in the design can be changed by varying the colors used.

**Color Key**

A  Red     B  Green     C  White

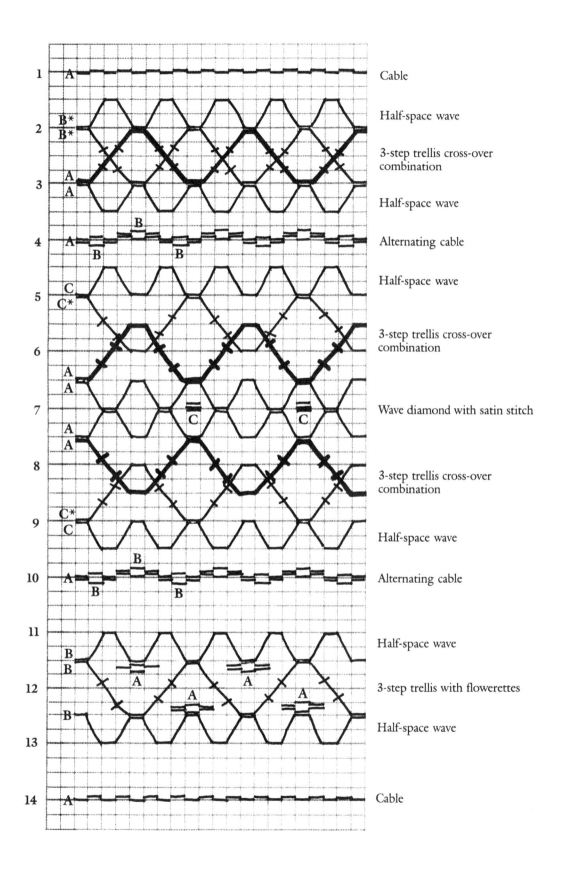

| Row | Pattern |
|---|---|
| 1 — A | Cable |
| 2 — B* B* | Half-space wave / 3-step trellis cross-over combination |
| 3 — A A | Half-space wave |
| 4 — A, B, B, B | Alternating cable |
| 5 — C C* | Half-space wave / 3-step trellis cross-over combination |
| 6 | |
| 7 — A A, C, C | Wave diamond with satin stitch |
| 8 — A A | 3-step trellis cross-over combination |
| 9 — C* C | Half-space wave |
| 10 — A, B, B, B | Alternating cable |
| 11 — B B | Half-space wave / 3-step trellis with flowerettes |
| 12 — A, A, B, A, A | Half-space wave |
| 13 | |
| 14 — A | Cable |

# Annabelle

**Rows 1½ to 2½ and 10 to 11:** With blue, work base rows of half-space cable-wave combination. With rose, work cross-over rows of half-space cable-wave combination.

## CENTER MOTIF

The small numbers indicate the order in which the rows are to be worked.

**Rows 5½ to 7½:** Beginning at Row 6½ with rose, work base rows of half-space trellis and 5-step trellis combination; then, with blue, complete the tops of the pyramids in half-space trellis as indicated by the dark lines on the graph.

**Cross-Over Rows:** Dark lines on graph. Beginning at Row 6 with blue, work a 5-step trellis up to Row 5, then work 7 cable stitches. Work an 8-step trellis down to Row 6½, picking up both the pleat and the thread of the base row. Work a half-space trellis, then an 8-step trellis back up to Row 5. Continue in this way across the row. Work Row 6½ to 8 in the same way.

**Row 6½:** Decorative stitches. Work a flowerette in each half-space trellis diamond.

**Color Key**

A   Blue      B   Rose

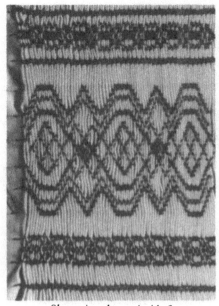

*Shown in color on inside front cover*

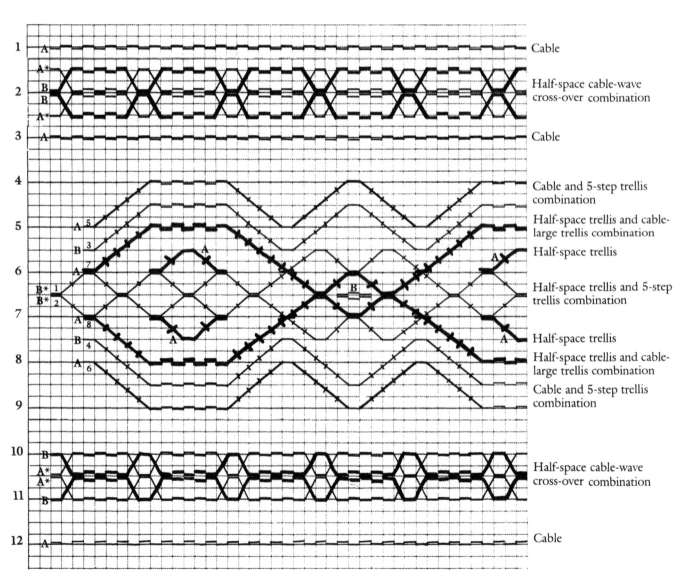

| Row | Label | Description |
|-----|-------|-------------|
| 1 | A | Cable |
| 2 | A* / B / B / A* | Half-space cable-wave cross-over combination |
| 3 | A | Cable |
| 4 | | Cable and 5-step trellis combination |
| 5 | A 5 / B 3 | Half-space trellis and cable-large trellis combination · Half-space trellis |
| 6 | A 7 | |
| 6½ | B* 1 / B* 2 | Half-space trellis and 5-step trellis combination |
| 7 | A 8 / B 4 | Half-space trellis |
| 8 | A 6 | Half-space trellis and cable-large trellis combination · Cable and 5-step trellis combination |
| 10 | B / A* / A* | Half-space cable-wave cross-over combination |
| 11 | B | |
| 12 | A | Cable |

34

# GROUP 3:
## PICTURE SMOCKING

### (*Advanced Skill*)

Picture smocking is a current favorite among those who practice decorative stitching. Through the arrangement of stitches and colors, forms such as bows or baskets, Santas or gingerbread men, butterflies or boats emerge across the pleated fabric.

This style of smocking requires excellent technical skills. As with any form of needlework, to attempt it before you are ready will be very frustrating. When you are prepared, you will discover a whole new avenue of design possibilities.

# Marguerite's Butterflies

*Shown in color on inside back cover*

**Rows 3½ to 5:** Decorative stitches. Work 2 bullion knots for each butterfly body. Use a blind tack stitch on the wrong side to hold the knots together. Work half-space trellis for the antennae. At the center of the butterfly wings (Row 4½) work flowerettes as indicated on graph.

**Rows 1½ to 3½ and Rows 5½ to 7½:** Decorative stitches. Work 2 satin stitches over 2 pleats as indicated on graph.

**Variations:** To form a larger design, add borders of trellis diamonds or open-space waves with cables above and below. Alternative color choices are green for background smocking and lavender and yellow for the butterflies, or else blue or brown for the background with yellow and green butterflies.

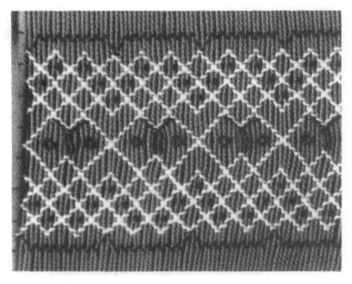

**Color Key**

A Navy     B Off-White

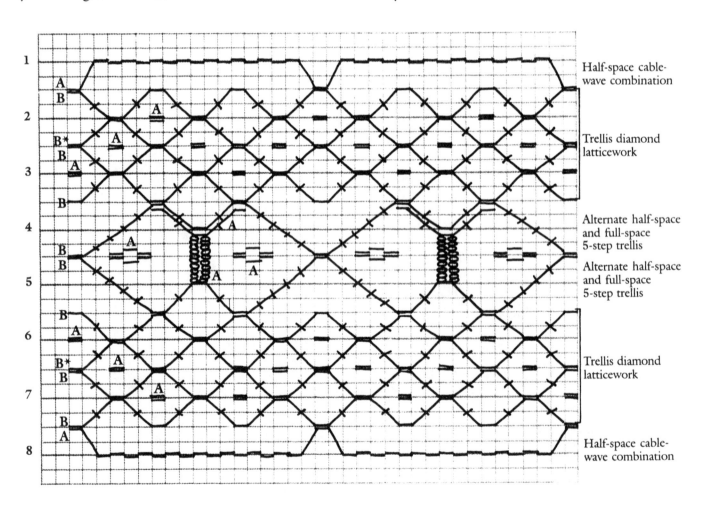

Half-space cable-wave combination

Trellis diamond latticework

Alternate half-space and full-space 5-step trellis

Alternate half-space and full-space 5-step trellis

Trellis diamond latticework

Half-space cable-wave combination

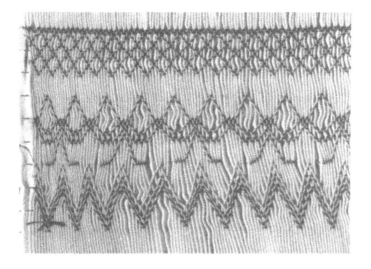

# Celina's Bow

*Shown in color on back cover*

## BOW MOTIF

Small numbers indicate the order in which to work the rows.

**Row 5 to 4:** Work 5-cable and 3-step full-space trellis combination.

**Row 5 to 5¾:** Work cable and 2-step trellis combination.

**Row 5¼ to 6:** Work 3-step trellis and 5-cable combination.

**Row 7 to 5½:** For streamers, work 4-step large trellis, working ends in stem stitch.

## Color Key

A  Dark Rose  
B  Medium Rose  
C  Light Rose  
D  Gray Blue

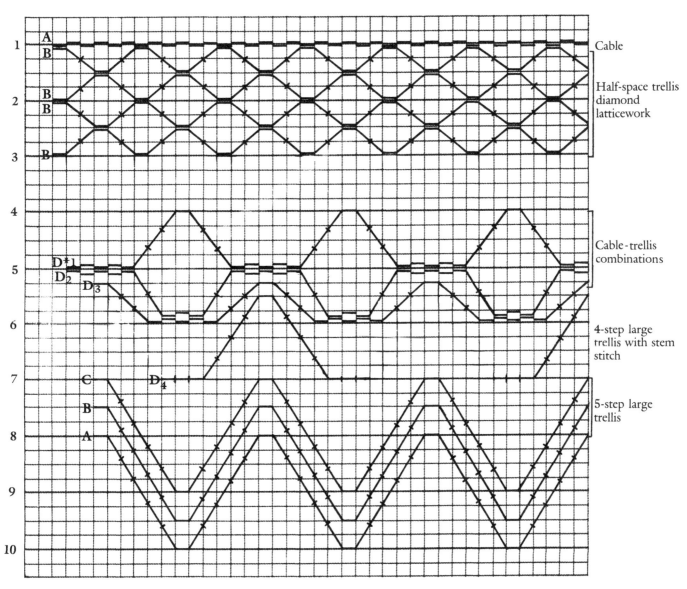

# ROSINA'S GARDEN

**Rows 4 to 5½:** The flowers are worked in opposite stacked cables and are shaded. Starting at the top on Row 4 and turning the work as necessary, work 3 cables with 3 strands of medium rose, 5 cables with 2 strands of light rose and 1 of medium rose, 7 cables with 3 strands of light rose, 9 cables with 2 strands of light rose and 1 of dark rose and 2 opposite rows of 11 cables with 3 strands of dark rose. Work the base of each flower in green.

**Row 6 to 5½:** Work satin-stitch bars for stems.

**Row 9 to 10:** Decorative stitches. Each rosebud is made of 3 bullion knots; the outer 2 knots in one color form the flower while the contrasting color knot forms the center. Work the colors in the following sequence:

*1. Outer knots, medium rose; center, dark rose.

2. Outer knots, light rose; center, medium rose.

3. Outer knots, dark rose; center, light rose.

Repeat from * across smocking. With each rosebud work a green lazy daisy stitch leaf.

**Variations:** This design may be divided into two separate designs with Rows 1–7 being one design and Rows 7–13 being another.

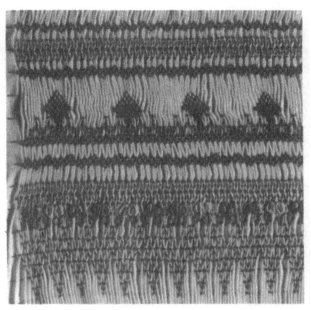

*Shown in color on inside front cover*

**Color Key**

| | | | |
|---|---|---|---|
| A | Medium Rose | C | Dark Rose |
| B | Light Rose | D | Green |

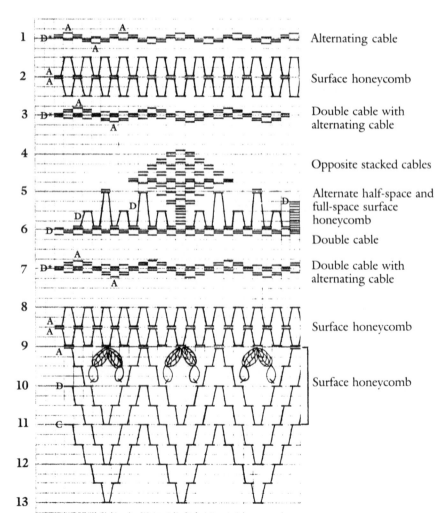

1 — Alternating cable

2 — Surface honeycomb

3 — Double cable with alternating cable

4 — Opposite stacked cables

5 — Alternate half-space and full-space surface honeycomb

6 — Double cable

7 — Double cable with alternating cable

8 — Surface honeycomb

9

10 — Surface honeycomb

11

12

13

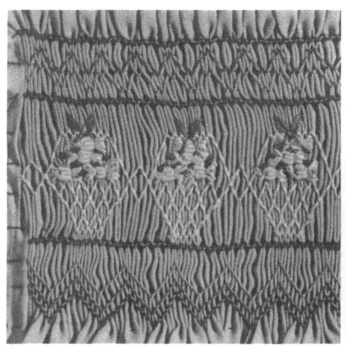
*Shown in color on inside back cover*

# Elena

**Row 5½ to 4 and Row 5½ to 6:** Work base row of half-space wave as indicated; then complete basket handles in half-space wave and cable-large trellis combination.

**Rows 6 to 7:** Pyramids to form bottom of basket. Work back and forth across each individual basket, turning work as necessary; do not carry thread across from basket to basket.

**Row 4 to 6:** Decorative stitches. In each basket work 4 bullion-knot rosebuds in dark yellow (each rosebud is made of 3 bullion knots). With green, add lazy daisy leaves to each flower, as shown on graph. With purple, scatter 6 or 7 French-knot buds about the flowers.

**Row 3 to 4:** Basket Bow. With lavender, work long lazy daisy stitches.

**Color Key**

| | | |
|---|---|---|
| A  Purple | C  Light Lavender | E  Dark Yellow |
| B  Lavender | D  Light Yellow | F  Green |

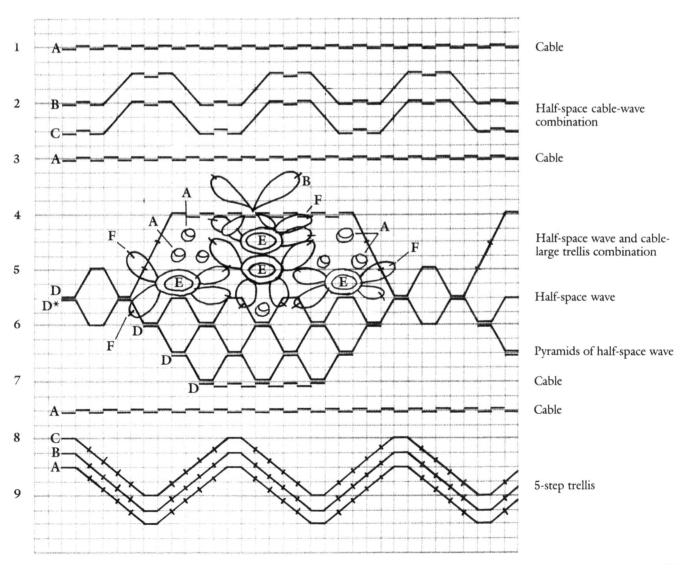

# Melody

*Shown in color on inside back cover*

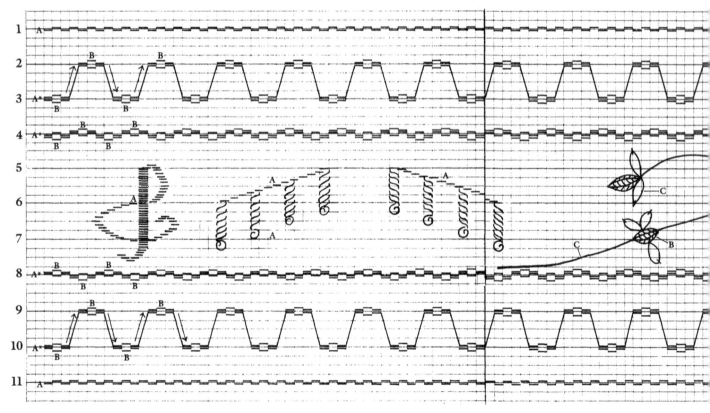

**Rows 2 to 3 and 9 to 10:** Work cable-wave combination with black. Work half-flowerettes in red, carrying thread on wrong side following arrows.

## CENTER MOTIF

This design must be centered.

**Bass Clef:** This motif covers 14 pleats. The bottom is satin stitch worked over 3 pleats, the central portion is satin stitch over 2 pleats, the horizontal base is outline stitch and the curved line is trellis stitch.

**Musical Notes:** Each note is worked in surface honeycomb stitch going up. The base of each note is a French knot worked with 4 strands of floss. The bar joining the notes is trellis stitch.

**Floral Design:** This free-form design is made up of bullion-stitch rosebuds with outline-stitch stems and lazy daisy stitch leaves.

### Color Key
A  Black      B  Red      C  Green

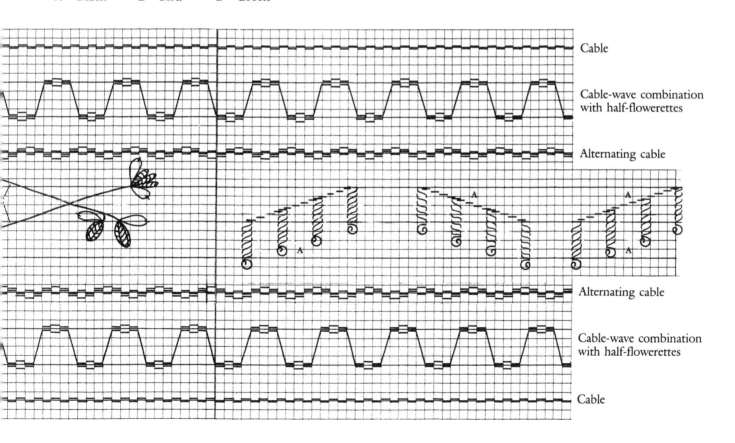

Cable

Cable-wave combination with half-flowerettes

Alternating cable

Alternating cable

Cable-wave combination with half-flowerettes

Cable

# Group 4:
## Advanced Designs

Experienced smockers will welcome the chance to try their hand at these lovely and intricate patterns. Through combinations of stitches and rows, shapes such as hearts, diamonds and pyramids appear across the pleated fabric. Rearrange the combinations, and old shapes emerge in new and different forms. In most cases, the central motif can be expanded by adding more rows.

# Katrina

*Shown in color on inside back cover*

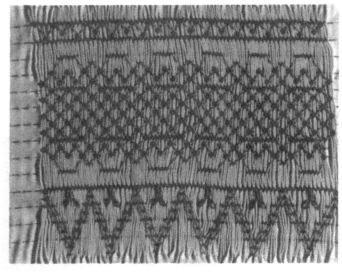

**Rows 1½ to 1¾, 4 to 4½ and 8½ to 9:** Decorative stitches. Spread pleats to desired finished width. Work half-flowerettes as indicated on graph, carrying thread loosely across back of work.

**Row 11 to 12:** Decorative stitches. Bullion-knot rosebuds are worked vertically; tack the completed knots to the fabric. Take a few backstitches on the wrong side of the fabric to keep pleats from separating.

**Variations:** This design may be used as is for a full yoke or Rows 1 through 10 may be used for a smaller yoke or an insert. The top border may also be repeated after Row 10. The bottom motif in Rows 11 through 15 may be used on a round yoke. To make it larger, add the border in Rows 1 and 2 above the bottom motif. Leave a full space before beginning the bottom motif.

**Color Key**

A  Blue     B  Green     C  Pink

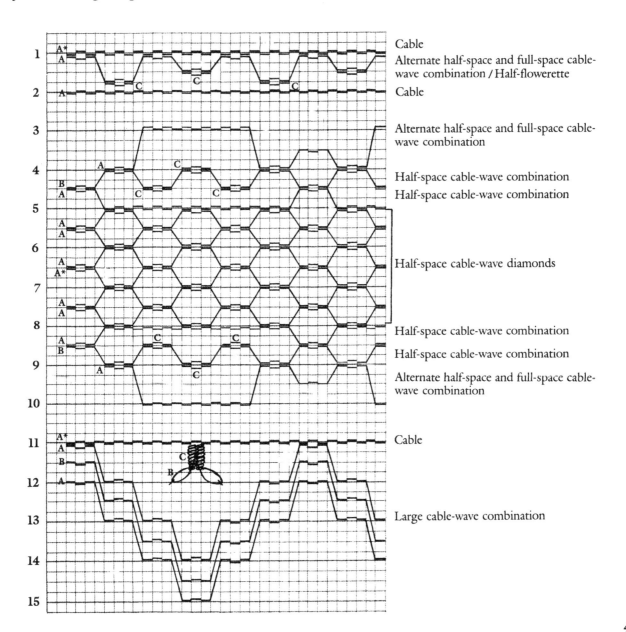

1 — Cable / Alternate half-space and full-space cable-wave combination / Half-flowerette

2 — Cable

3 — Alternate half-space and full-space cable-wave combination

4 — Half-space cable-wave combination / Half-space cable-wave combination

5, 6, 7 — Half-space cable-wave diamonds

8 — Half-space cable-wave combination / Half-space cable-wave combination

9 — Alternate half-space and full-space cable-wave combination

11 — Cable

13 — Large cable-wave combination

# Springtime

*Shown in color on inside back cover*

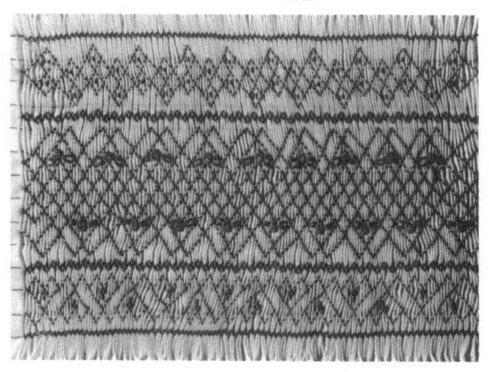

This design illustrates asymmetrical patterns and the way to carry threads across the back of the work. The threads are carried on the back either up and down or at a slight angle. Follow the small numbers on the graph. The motifs may be smocked in one color, or the top and bottom areas may be in different colors. If more than one color is used in the bottom motif, the shapes will not show up the same.

## TOP MOTIF

**Rows 2½ to 2 and 2½ to 3:** Work base rows of half-space trellis.

**Row 3 to 3½:** Work in half-space trellis.

**Rows 2 to 1½ and 3½ to 4:** Work alternating half-space trellis at the top and bottom as follows: Secure the thread at 1 and work half-space trellis to 2. Carry the yarn on the wrong side to 3, then work a half-space trellis to 4. Carry the thread to 5 and work from 5 to 6. Continue in this way across the row.

**Rows 2 to 3½:** In diamonds, work 2 satin stitches over 2 pleats as indicated by curved lines on graph.

## CENTER MOTIF

**Rows 6½ to 9:** Work rows of half-space trellis to form latticework.

**Row 6½ to 5½:** Work alternate half-space trellis and full-space, 5-step trellis.

**Row 6 to 5:** Work alternate full-space, 5-step trellis and half-space trellis.

**Rows 6 and 9:** Decorative stitches. Work bullion-knot rose buds with matching French-knot center; add lazy daisy stitch leaves.

## BOTTOM MOTIF

**Rows 12 to 11½ and 13 to 13½:** Work half-space trellis.

**Row 12 to 13:** Secure thread at 1 and work a 5-step trellis to 2. Carry thread on wrong side to 3, then work a 5-step trellis to 4. Carry thread on wrong side to 5. Continue in this way across the row.

**Rows 12 to 13:** Decorative stitches. Work flowerettes and satin stitches as indicated on graph.

### COLOR KEY
A  Pink    B  Green

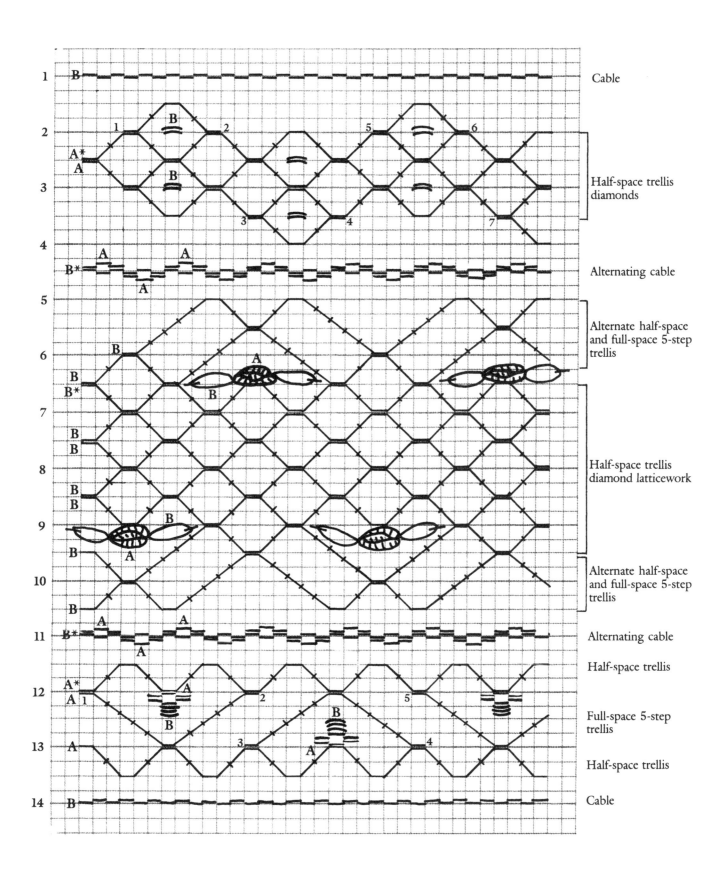

1 · B — Cable

2 · 1 B 2 5 B 6 ⎤
A* ⎪
A ⎬ Half-space trellis
3 · B 3 4 7 ⎦ diamonds

4 · A A
B* ⎯ Alternating cable
A

5 · ⎤ Alternate half-space
⎪ and full-space 5-step
6 · B A ⎦ trellis
B B
B* ⎤
7 · B ⎪
B ⎪
8 · B ⎬ Half-space trellis
B ⎪ diamond latticework
9 · B ⎪
A ⎦
B ⎤ Alternate half-space
10 · ⎬ and full-space 5-step
B ⎦ trellis

11 · A A
B* ⎯ Alternating cable
A
— Half-space trellis
12 · A* A
A 1 2 5 — Full-space 5-step
B trellis
13 · A 3 B 4 — Half-space trellis
A

14 · B — Cable

# Pink Polonaise

*Shown in color on inside back cover*

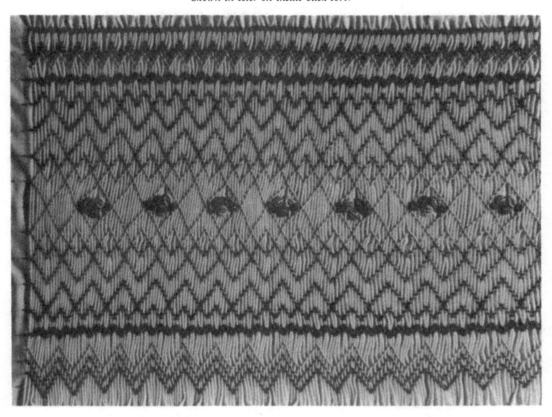

This is a basic design using half-space trellis and large 5-step trellis stitches to form waves, hearts and diamonds. It is an exercise in shading, with the choice of color determining the appearance of the different shapes. The design can also be done all in one color. A dark color will emphasize all the hearts.

**Row 8:** Decorative stitches. Three bullion-knot rosebuds are worked in every other diamond across.

Make individual buds of 3 bullion knots each—one shade of rose for outer knots and a contrasting shade of rose for the center. For leaves, work 2 green lazy daisy stitches.

**Color Key**

| | |
|---|---|
| A  Dark Rose | C  Light Rose |
| B  Medium Rose | D  Green |

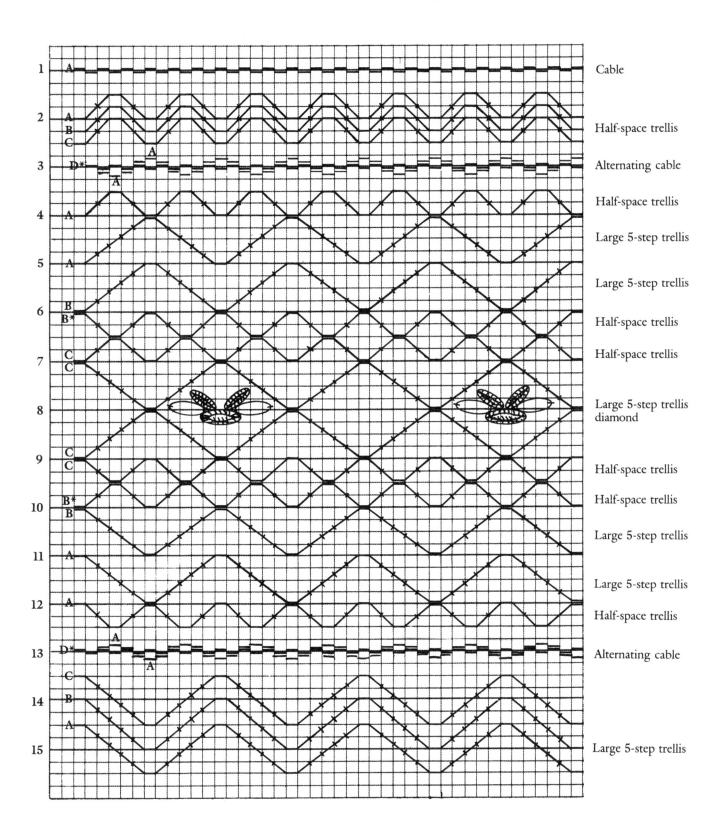

1    A                               Cable

2    A B C               Half-space trellis

3    D*      A          Alternating cable

      A                  Half-space trellis

4    A                    Large 5-step trellis

5    A                    Large 5-step trellis

6    B B*               Half-space trellis

7    C C               Half-space trellis

8                         Large 5-step trellis diamond

9    C C               Half-space trellis

10   B* B              Half-space trellis

                             Large 5-step trellis

11   A                    Large 5-step trellis

12   A                    Half-space trellis

13   D*     A          Alternating cable

14   C B A            

15                             Large 5-step trellis

# Madeira Lace

**Row 3 to 2:** Decorative stitches. Half-flowerettes: Follow arrows to carry thread across back of work. Work Row 12 to 13 in same manner.

**Row 5 to 6½:** Work a half-flowerette at top of cable-trellis combination, then carry thread across back of work to bottom of cable-trellis combination and work rose portion of opposite stacked cable, turning the work as necessary. Carry thread across back of work to be in position for next half-flowerette. When the row is complete, go back and work the pink portion of the opposite stacked cable, but do not carry the pink thread across the back of the work. Work remaining similar rows in the same manner.

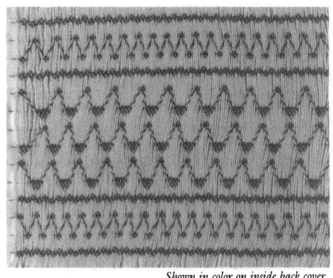

*Shown in color on inside back cover*

## Color Key

A   Green        B   Rose        C   Pink

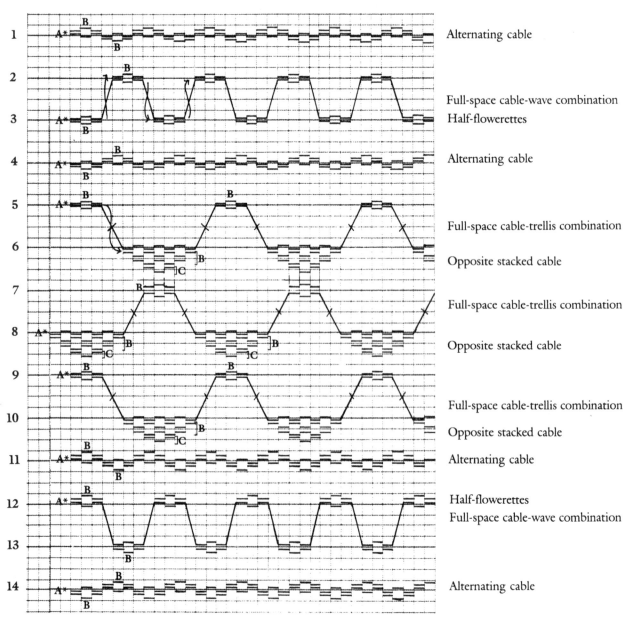

1    Alternating cable

2    Full-space cable-wave combination
3    Half-flowerettes

4    Alternating cable

5    Full-space cable-trellis combination

6    Opposite stacked cable

7    Full-space cable-trellis combination

8    Opposite stacked cable

9    Full-space cable-trellis combination

10   Opposite stacked cable

11   Alternating cable

12   Half-flowerettes
     Full-space cable-wave combination

13

14   Alternating cable